CW00448105

Self-Portrait in the Dark

Colette Bryce was born in Derry in 1970 and
emigrated to England when she was eighteen.
She has lived in London, Spain and Scotland
and is currently based in Newcastle upon Tyne
where she works as a freelance writer and editor.

Also by Colette Bryce

The Heel of Bernadette
The Full Indian Rope Trick
The Observations of Aleksandr Svetlov

Colette Bryce

Self-Portrait in the Dark

PICADOR

First published 2008 by Picador

This edition published 2016 by Picador
an imprint of Pan Macmillan, a division of Macmillan Publishers Limited
Pan Macmillan, 20 New Wharf Road, London N1 9RR
Associated companies throughout the world
www.panmacmillan.com

ISBN 978-5098-3908-7

Copyright © Colette Bryce 2008

The right of Colette Bryce to be identified as the
author of this work has been asserted by her in accordance
with the Copyright, Designs and Patents Act 1988.

Picador has no responsibility for the information
provided by and author websites whose address you obtain from
this book ('author websites'). The inclusion of author website
addresses in this book does not constitute an endorsement by or
association with us of such sites or the content, products,
advertising or other materials presented on such sites.

All rights reserved. No part of this publication may be
reproduced, stored in or introduced into a retrieval system, or
transmitted, in any form, or by any means (electronic, mechanical,
photocopying, recording or otherwise) without the prior written
permission of the publisher. Any person who does any unauthorized
act in relation to this publication may be liable to criminal
prosecution and civil claims for damages.

A CIP catalogue record for this book is available from
the British Library.

Printed and bound by CPI Group (UK) Ltd, Croydon, CR0 4YY

This book is sold subject to the condition that it shall not,
by way of trade or otherwise, be lent, re-sold, hired out,
or otherwise circulated without the publisher's prior consent
in any form of binding or cover other than that in which
it is published and without a similar condition including this
condition being imposed on the subsequent purchaser.

Visit www.picador.com to read more about all our books
and to buy them. You will also find features, author interviews and
news of any author events, and you can sign up for e-newsletters
so that you're always first to hear about our new releases.

for Úna Bryce

A house can be haunted by those who were never there.

LOUIS MACNEICE

Acknowledgements

A number of these poems first appeared in the
following publications: *Answering Back* (Picador),
Art World, *Best of Irish Poetry 2007* (Southword),
Big Issue Cymru, *Blinking Eye*, *Daily Mirror*,
Evansville Review, *New Welsh Review*, *Poetry
London*, *Poetry Review*, *Pratik*, *Stinging Fly*,
The Ropes (Diamond Twig).

'Self-Portrait in a Broken Wing-Mirror' won first
prize in the Cardiff International Poetry Competition
2007.

I would like to acknowledge the support of the
Universities of Newcastle and Durham and the Arts
Council of England through my appointment to the
North East Literary Fellowship 2005–07; and to
thank my editor Don Paterson for his good advice.

Contents

Self-Portrait in the Dark

A Spider

I trapped a spider in a glass,
a fine-blown wineglass.
It shut around him, silently.
He stood still, a small wheel
of intricate suspension, cap
at the hub of his eight spokes,
inked eyes on stalks; alert,
sensing a difference.
I meant to let him go
but still he taps against the glass
all Marcel Marceau
in *the wall that is there but not there*,
a circumstance I know.

Self-Portrait in the Dark (with Cigarette)

To sleep, perchance
to dream? No chance:
it's 4 a.m. and I'm wakeful
as an animal,
caught between your presence and the lack.
This is the realm insomniac.
On the window seat, I light a cigarette
from a slim flame and monitor the street –
a stilled film, bathed in amber,
softened now in the wake of a downpour.

Beyond the daffodils
on Magdalen Green, there's one slow vehicle
pushing its beam along Riverside Drive,
a sign of life;
and two months on
from 'moving on'
your car, that you haven't yet picked up,
waits, spattered in raindrops like bubble wrap.
Here, I could easily go off
on a riff

on how cars, like pets, look a little like their owners
but I won't 'go there',
as they say in America,
given it's a clapped-out Nissan Micra . . .
And you don't need to know that
I've been driving it illegally at night
in the lamp-lit silence of this city
– you'd only worry –
or, worse, that Morrissey
is jammed in the tape deck now and for eternity;

no. It's fine, all gleaming hubcaps,
seats like an upright, silhouetted couple;
from the dashboard, the wink
of that small red light I think
is a built-in security system.
In a poem
it could represent a heartbeat or a pulse.
Or loneliness: its vigilance.
Or simply the lighthouse-regular spark
of someone, somewhere, smoking in the dark.

Car Wash

This business of driving
reminds us of our fathers.
The low purr of fifth gear,
the sharp fumes, the biscuity
interior – has brought them,
ever-absent, nearer.
And has brought us, two
women in our thirties,
to this strange pass,
a car wash in Belfast;
where we've puzzled
and opted for 'Executive
Service' (meaning
detergent) and have minded
the instructions to wind up
our windows and sit
tight when the red light
shows, and find ourselves
delighted by a wholly
unexpected privacy
of soap suds pouring, no,
cascading in velvety waves.

And when spinning blue brushes
of implausible dimensions
are approaching the vehicle
from all directions,
what can we do
but engage in a kiss
in a world where to do so
can still stop the traffic.

And then to the rinse,
and in view once again
of incurious motorists
idling on the forecourt,
we are polished and finished
and (following instructions)
start the ignition (which
reminds us of our fathers)
and get into gear
and we're off
at the green light.

The Knack

Place yourself
between the tracks, lie

as you would occupy
a grave – arms

crossed on chest, eyes
closed, deep

breath – and the life
will thunder over.

Wait through screech
and wheeze of brakes,

billow of smoke,
dust, heat,

for a settling.
Get to your feet.

If a hand is offered
from above, take it

with good grace; climb
back into the afternoon

and the next phase.

The Residents

Opening the door requires the breaking of a web
then spores of something in the air jab
at your throat. Your cough disturbs
an absence shaped to the room's contours.
You walk to a window silvered with a mist
that might be the breath of a captive ghost
and open the catch, admitting a gust
that rouses the papers, raises the dust.

Bunker, funk-hole, new-place-to-dwell,
the mould is blossoming on the wall.

A column of ants advancing on the carpet
swerves to avoid a rodent pellet.
An ancient terminal squats on the desk
resolutely incompatible with current systems.
Shyly, you occupy the swivel chair
which sinks by inches, open a drawer
where her pens collected year upon year
with brown coins, fluff, and hair.

Bunker, funk-hole, new-place-to-dwell,
the mould is blossoming on the wall.

You have entered the mind of the previous incumbent,
chaos, yes, but rationally governed
by a certain Havisham imperative.
You have come, like her, to 'be creative'
and 'encourage creativity', for your sins.
The radiator fills with clunks and groans.

Is this a crime-scene? Is it a shrine?
You check the phone for an outside line.

Bunker, funk-hole, new-place-to-dwell,
the mould is blossoming on the wall.

If asked, you could offer a team from forensics:
– various punched-out blister packs
– a fingerprint in a lip-gloss compact
– a half-smoked menthol cigarette
– a woollen scarf unravelling on a hook
– a mildewed draft of her second book
– a culture thriving in her unwashed cup
– a single plimsoll, size five, lace-up

Bunker, funk-hole, new-place-to-dwell,
the mould is blossoming on the wall.

and posit a case of spontaneous combustion
perhaps, or an extraterrestrial abduction . . .
But the thought stalls, skips three years
to a bright young novelist opening the door;
the inaudible snap of a spider's thread
as he takes his first steps into your head.

The Hunted

Fugitive in the wrong century, shadowy,
how frail he looks, how stooped,
wrapped in a blue translucence.

Easing slowly into stasis,
pacing out the days in frames;
the golden winter light is like forgiveness.

Nothing connects.
All is a matter of words. He is not
what he used to be. He is interested now

in birds, and botany, cricket . . . Sorry,
can we speak up please? He can't
quite catch what it is we are saying.

Self-Portrait in a Broken Wing-Mirror

The lens has popped from its case,
minutely cracked and yet intact, tilted
where it stopped against a rock on the tarmac.
And this could be Selkirk, washed up on a beach,
in prone position surveying the sweep
of his future sanctuary, or prison.

But no, that's me, a cubist depiction: my ear,
its swirl and ridge of pearly cartilage,
peachy lobe and indent of a piercing
not jewelled for years. I punctured that
with a nerve of steel at fifteen in a bolted
room. It was Hallowe'en. I had no fear.

The ear is parted neatly from the head
by breaks in the glass, a weird mosaic
or logic puzzle for the brain to fix.
The eyebrow, stepped in sections, stops
then starts again, recognisably mine.
The nose, at an intersection of cracks,

is all but lost except for the small sculpted
cave of a shadowy nostril. The eye
is locked on itself, the never-easy gaze
of the portraitist, the hood half open,
the hub of the pupil encircled with green
and a ring of flame. I have make-up on,

a smudging of pencil, brushed black lashes.
I'd swear the face looks younger than before,
the skin sheer, the fine wires of laughter
disappeared without the animation.
The lips are slack, pink, segmented;
a slight gravitational pull towards the earth

gives the upper one a sort of Elvis curl.
The same effect has made the cheek more full.
I have never been so still. A beautiful day
and not another car for what seems like hours.
Also in the glass, bisected, out of focus,
a streamer of road and a third of sky.

Presently, I will attempt to move,
attempt to arise in a shower of diamonds,
but first I must finish this childish contest
where one must stare the other out, not look
away, like a painting in a gallery, where
only the blink of an eye might restart time.

On Highgate Hill

It is late July and Coleridge is dead.

The funeral cortège
snakes its way along the road.
Locals loiter by the hedgerows,
hands joined, heads bowed,
hats clasped to chests.
Porlock steps aside with all the rest.

It filters through the gates of Highgate Church.

It narrows through the doorway's solemn arch.

What else?
Selected words are said.
A box is lowered into earth.
Mourners gradually disperse
like images on the surface of a stream
into which a stone is cast.

On Not Finding the Angelry

We lower our sights and sit at the edge
of the trees and listen
and listening see
they are perched, at roost in the high branches,
infant-sized and goblin-lithe.

Some have their wings held out to dry
like sea witches;
coos and calls
ring out like notes from whittled flutes
amplified in the woods' acoustic.

Every so often, a small commotion
shakes the peace:
an Earhart or Icarus
crashes softly through the canopy,
settles safe on a platform nest –

a crown of sticks – and folds its wings,
hunkers down,
hugs its chest
and shuts its amber lantern eyes
the better to rest itself for the night.

Or one breaks out like a dove from a top hat
or a shout
or a panicked thought
and is gone. It might have never been.
We close our scopes and start for home.

Finisterre

Nothing to do in this place
but turn and return, or stop
and look out into nothing;
ocean and sky in a blue
confusion, the curved shriek
of a gull.

       Nothing to catch
the wind but a tourist's hair,
her summer linens blown,
her palm to the granite
cross, a squint smile
for a husband's camera flash.

   *

Sun, after days of loose
Galician rain, is siphoning
moisture from the stone
of the afternoon, while shadows
creep by increments
from under the flowers,
their little hoods and bells
frail, incongruous in the rocks.

   *

Just visible, at the foot
of the cliffs, a tiny vessel,
stopped, at anchor; a thin
figure lowering lines
and basket traps to the depths.

The great lamp sleeps my heart
my heart is contracting
after light. Aloneness
is the word I was looking for.

Next Year's Luck

Next year's luck (now we're seeking it)
clings on stubborn to the upper limbs.

We reach, as children might for snow.
It is orange, crumpled, red, gold

and the unpindownable colours of flames
(new luck always manifests as old)

it is shrivelled, tindery, crisp and so
so delicate that touch might destroy it.

We have walked three seasons to be here
to watch it fall like tongues of fire

but next year's luck is taking its time
floating, meandering into our lives,

uncatchable; then sticking to our boots
and decomposing, nourishing the roots.

One Night in the Glasgow Central Hotel

In the Interim Bar, the no longer hopeful
drink to get drunk in a harsh light,
in a bastion of fading grandeur.
The night is neither young nor over.

The resident ghosts look out into Hope Street
and do not disturb.

Confused by a maze of lamplit corridors,
you opt for the opulent mirrored lift
and stand at one remove from yourself,
confronting the back of your own head.

The resident ghosts look out into Hope Street
and do not disturb.

The room has a carpety-cushioning effect,
no edge off which a sound might resonate;
greyish nets, the familiar airlessness,
a planet's televisual detritus.

The resident ghosts look out into Hope Street
and do not disturb.

Brown bathwater forces you to think
of something decomposing in the tank
that can't be disguised by an extra sachet
of Morning Mist or a clam-shaped soap.

The resident ghosts look out into Hope Street
and do not disturb.

Dawn, and you're frantically trying to locate
the Gideon Bible in the bedside cabinet,
indexed for fearfulness, drug-abuse, despair,
having dreamed that dream of eternal corridors.

*The resident ghosts look out into Hope Street
and do not disturb.*

And no, you never checked out in the end
but walk and walk those muted halls
searching for breakfast – for *kippers on request,*
the bar, a payphone, human contact . . .

*The resident ghosts look out into Hope Street
and do not disturb.*

Ghost Words

Forever around the next corner,
stressing the stairs, stopped
at the foot, I'm just out of sight,
just out of earshot.

My dead call
is a lead ball rolled
through a tunnel of empty rooms.

Bored, I worry
the Gallery, absently pick out
three small notes
on the baby grand: *plink plink plink*.

My fingers riffle
the crystal tears of a chandelier,
an audible shiver.

I float through a door,
you prick up your ears. I pass
through your body, front
to back, like a sigh,
a faint electric shock.

You lean to your work, I raise
the downy hairs on your neck,
you shift and shudder.

I pull up a pew, pretend
to be you with your life's blood
but it's no good.

I fold myself into the wall
and am gone. The scrape of my chair
on the floor echoes on.

Twelve

We took a zigzag route along a scrawl of narrow, stony roads
that cut across the peaty fens, bleak
at this time of year.

We pulled over, stretched, gathered. Someone had propped
a small bouquet of freesias at the start
of the track, and a card

'we have you in our hearts'. We walked slowly, awkwardly,
like a hushed procession in a church,
conscious of our hands.

There was mud on the ground and trees on either side and a
    mess
of undergrowth. A waist-high broken branch
where a strand of hair

had snagged, was pointed out. A clearing where a vehicle,
conceivably, could have turned around.
An opening where a man

could have left the track and reached the hidden ditch, six
    hundred
paces from the road. I focused on the guide
in front, burs clinging

to his coat. And then the spot. The remnants of a cordon
were fluttering in a light breeze. 'Feel free . . .'
Silently, we looked at it.

The Hopes

They extend above the houses
like mechanical giraffes.

Dignified,
they are there for a reason.

Cables hang
from their heads like harnesses.

Behind them, the sky is unusually
blue and clear

for a month so late
in the year. Don't give up.

Where Are You?

I'd guess
in a supermarket,
from the backing track of barcode bleeps
and the jerk-squeaky wheel
of a trolley, audible
on the phone.

At a distance, a child
bawls, its open mouth a black
hole into which the earth itself
might fall.

You speak in a confidential tone,
moving through the aisles,
your eye selecting
certain items.

*

You ring me back
from the car park, sitting
in your window-bubble.
In the boot, plastic bags settle
with a faint crackle.

The denizens of outer space
float about their business
or slowly drift away.

Earthbound,
I'm losing you.
There's not the reach on the line.
Somewhere in the universe
your voice is breaking up again.

Nature Walk

If only my bag had been large enough,
I would have brought the lonely men in parked cars
by the river. I would have brought the woman
dabbing kohl tears with the heel
of her hand. I might have brought the ancient couple
who read each word on the YOU ARE HERE
board, then turned and ambled on, heads
a little upward-tilted, showing
an interest in everything.

I would have brought the coping-stone
from the twelfth pier of the original bridge, and the 4:06
from elsewhere, curving (glittering) carefully across.
And all the busy people on it; all their coats
and phones and wallets. I might
have brought the restless gulls that dropped
like paper boats on to the water. And the burger van,
the girl inside with greasy hair,
her quite unsolvable crossword.

And put them all on my nature table,
and fashioned little cardboard signs:
a small display that would speak in a way
about loneliness and life spans, parked cars and rivers.

I brought some bark, and a couple of conkers,
one still half-encased in its skin like an eye.

Vertical Blinds

Vertical blinds
stand sentry at her life
switch on a whim
to admit or refuse light.
World outside
is presented in stripes.
Vertical blinds
stand sentry at her life.
Puppet- compliant
at the tugging of a string
how quick they flip
to a cinema screen's
oriental projection
pale afternoon
phantom branches
interrupting sun.
Vertical blinds

stand sentry at her life
bars of a cage
taut strips of bandage
gripped with a clip
at top and tail
they are sails of ships
a fleet that will lift
carry her far
from all of this.
But they change tack
bearing her back
to the masked gloom
of a living- room.
Vertical blinds
stand sentry at her life
switch on a whim
to admit or refuse light.

When I Land in Northern Ireland

When I land in Northern Ireland I long for cigarettes,
for the blue plume of smoke hitting the lung with a thud and,
   God,
the quickening blood as the stream administers the nicotine.
Stratus shadows darkening the crops
when coming in to land,
coming in to land.

What's your poison?
A question in a bar
draws me down through a tunnel of years
to a time preserved in a cube of fumes, the seventies-yellowing
walls of remembrance; everyone smokes and talks about the
   land,
the talk about the land, our spoiled inheritance.

The Harm

On the walk to school you have stopped
at the one significant lamppost, just to be sure
(if you're late where's the harm?),
and are tracing the cut of the maker's name in raised print
and yes, you are certain it is still ticking,
softly ticking where it stands on the corner

opposite McCaul's corner-
shop. Not that you had expected it to stop.
At worst, all you'll get from the teacher is a good ticking
off. When it goes off, and you are sure
it will be soon, this metal panel with its neat square print
will buckle like the lid of Pandora's tin and harm

will blow from the mechanical heart, harm
in a wild cacophony of colour. A car takes the corner
as you start to cross and the driver's face imprints
itself on your mind forever, a whitened mask, as he stops
a hair's breadth from the sure
and quickened ticking

of your child's heart – a little clock or timer ticking.
'For God's sake stay on the pavement out of harm's
way!' the woman who grabs you says. 'Sure
haven't you been told how to cross a road? This corner
has already seen the death of my daughter. Stop
and look, and look both ways!' She prints

her grip on your thin bare arm, the sour imprint
of alcohol on her too-close breath. Then the ticking
of a wheel, as a man on a bicycle slows to a stop,
dismounts, and tells her 'It's okay Mary, there's no harm
done.' He leads her from the corner,
talking in her ear, 'It's alright Mary. Yes, yes, I am sure.'

He motions with his eyes for you to leave but, unsure,
you wait, frozen by the lamppost, the lettering print-
ing ridges in your palm, until you run at last to the
    opposite corner
and walk to the school, the woman's words still ticking
in your head, her notion of harm
and the thought of her daughter, unable to stop

missing school. You are sure, as sure as the ticking
lamppost is a bomb, its timer on, of harm, printed
forever on the corner where the woman's world has stopped.

Negotiating the Muse

Clocking you across a room
I leave immediately.

I feign disinterest
at your latest news

and live abroad
just to avoid you.

Flights arc
like stitches between us.

Awareness
can be a dreadful thing.

Out on the town
you are spilling your guts

to the latest in a line
of Johnny-come-latelys.

I bite my lip
and observe, discreetly.

Meeting you
would horrify.

You are nothing like
what I have in mind.

Volcanoes

The fine, wrought-iron furniture
is adult-sized yet somehow miniature,
painted a pine or a racing green;
and our hostess could be the new Monroe
wearing the face from a framed-up poster
hung in the lab of my science teacher
all those lives ago
who would clamp her palm like a gag on the smile
to show us the anger in the eyes.

Next to the murmuring guests, a child
is lying, stretched out on the lawn,
for the child has learned of the curvature
of the earth and is listening for the core,
the core that sounds like an old gas fire,
quiet, yet persistent, *there*,
the roar of isolated flame –
impossible – then a mind ablaze,
a mind ablaze with a deep unease.

The earth has vents, I tell the child,
vents release and vents restrain.
Safety. We look to the skies
for the black of the void with its billion eyes.
For the sky is the mind that grew to birth
the core and the layers and the crust of the earth.
The mind in the cavern of the skull.
The skull the limits of the skies.
The core in the dark behind the eyes.

34

Sin Música

The words cover more than they reveal.
I lift these lines from your virtual letter.

How short they fall
of real meaning. Your actual

touch was so much better
than words. I cover more than I reveal,

I know, but you were clear and cool
as air, and love a catar-

act or waterfall
into real meaning, simple

truth I fail to utter
in words that cover more than they reveal;

or the lifeless font of electronic mail,
here, at the point where it does not matter

how short they fall
of real meaning. Habitual,

I rearrange this useless clutter
of words, words;

words that cover more than they reveal.
How short they fall.

Seven in Bed

(Louise Bourgeois)

A muddle of thick limbs like a knot
of sausages in a butcher's window.
It is night here, they are trying to sleep.
It is morning. They are awakening, yawning.
Pink as meat on a sheet of white,
they are seven in bed, and nothing
is quite what it seems. Two-headed,
Janus-faced, are they clinging to each other
or trying to escape? Their stitched seams
have a rawness, surgical. Long groans
attest to a struggle. Prisoners.
They are like wrestlers in a scrum.
Is it love? Do they love each other?

Large Winged Vessel

(Colin Pearson)

If the large winged vessel
in the lit glass case,
short and squat
on its flat stone base,
is more like a coal bucket
weighted to a hearth
than an entity likely
to lift off from the earth

what does it matter?
If you lean in close
you may tune to its dream
of a better life than this –
to be raised by the ears
by the captain of a team
to the rousing cheers
of a stadium.

But knowing it may never leave
the bright glass case,
it sits, not centred
but back towards a corner
like a boxer surveying
his square of fighting space.
The large winged vessel
is putting on a brave face.

The Manager

The office after dark shifts
in a streetlamp atmospheric,
a cornery mind
turned in on itself,
seeming to find
a quietness.

Blinds hang at half mast.
Closed door. Shut drawers.
Strip-bulbs slumber
in their casings.
The radiator cools in pangs.

Seen from out there in the night,
it is a note extinguished
in the skyline.

Inside is an amber spell,
a window's Rothko-repeat
on the opposite wall.

Hard footsteps fade
in the echoey corridor.

An anglepoise in silhouette
suspends above the desk
in a short-sighted scrutiny,
a hermit's hood or bell.

That cabinet, the heart, boom
boom, with its hoard
of duplicates.

The terminal, a squat god,
is expressionless,
its pinpoint pulse
evidence
of something else.

The chair creaks on its stalk, its foot
an asterisk on castors.
Why is he sitting
there in the dark
in any case?
Perhaps he's lost it.

The bucket of black is only a bin,
a bluish gleam around the rim.

The scribble of leads at his feet,
though it seems to writhe, is not
a pit of snakes.

Get up. Go home.
It is time for the setting
of alarms, for codes and keypads,
hairspring triggers.

A sudden sweep illumination:
the swift cloth of headlights
wiping the walls,
then gone.

From the street, the clatter
of shutters going down.

The Poetry Bug

is a moon-pale, lumpish creature
parcelled in translucent skin
papery as filo pastry
patterned faint as a fingerprint
is quite without face or feature
ear or eye or snout
has eight root-like
tentacles or feelers, rough
like knuckly tusks of ginger
clustered at the front.

Invisible to the naked eye
monstrous in microscopy
it loves the lovers' bed or couch
pillow, quilt or duvet
and feeds, *thrives* I should say
on human scurf and dander
indeed, is never happier
than feasting on the dust
of love's shucked husk
the micro-detritus of us.

Once

Some words you may use only once.
Repeat them to some newer heart
and all your accuracy is gone.
                              Denise Riley

Sweetheart, darling. Years on,
how the old terms fail;
words that we loved with, once.

Older, on our second chance,
we stand, faltering hearts
in hands, inaccurate

and passionate, in love's
late, unfurnished rooms,
full of the words we cannot use;

and drive home, the same
streets, drop through the gears
to steer around the gone

words, the known
words, the beautiful outworn
words, those we may use only once,
all our accuracy gone.

Belfast Waking, 6 a.m.

A maintenance man
in a small white van attends
to the city's empty confessionals,
wipes glass walls and pincers litter
(the crisp polystyrene casing
of a burger) like evidence
of the utmost significance,

wrinkles his nose at the tang of urine,
furrows his brow at a broken syringe
then finally turns to the stoical machine,

the dangling receiver's plaintive refrain
*please replace the handset
and try again,*

unclogs the coin-choked gullet with a tool
and a little force
like a shoulder to a wheel
or an act of necessary violence.

Sites of anonymous threat
or sanctuary, they are out of place
in the cool new century,
but he likes the way

they continue to protect
their odd rectangular blocks of light
whether the people visit them or not.

Above his head, everything is changing;
black diluting
into the blue of a morning's
infinitely slow expression.

The gradual realisation of a steeple, a ripple
of birdsong on the surface of the dawn,
a dawn that is breaking its heart over Belfast.

Béal Feirste. Redbrick terraces. Tightrope wires
and telegraph poles. The liquid slink
of a feline or a fox, one gutter
to the other, then under a fence.

A refuse vehicle's cavernous jaw
reverses massively out of an avenue,
its amber, interrupted beam
glancing hatchbacks stationed in a line.

Footsteps nearing, footsteps fading.
An upturned collar, the clearing of a throat.
A muffled *whump* as a car door shuts.
Its smooth ignition.

The moment, precise,
when the streetlamps of Belfast
quietly go out, a unanimous decision,
and the windowpanes start filling up with sky
at the advent of the ordinary
business of the day.

Espresso

A minuscule bird
clinging to a twig

is shredding a loop
of knotted string

to a fibre-fuzzy
mist in its bill,

a haze as soft
as cotton wool

with which to line
a nest no bigger

than this small cup
I lift to my lips

while I wait for you
in this little coffee shop

on the avenue,
for such is April.

picador.com

blog
videos
interviews
extracts